Men Don't Marry For Sex

Men Don't Marry For Sex

Robert Hustrulid, M.D.

ISBN: 978-1-4993-8130-6

Printed in the United States of America

Contents

Chapter 1

Introductory Remarks

What Is This Book All About?

IT'S BEEN SAID that the most important decision we make in our lives is who we marry. The intent of this work is to try to figure out why we marry the people we marry and why it frequently becomes an unsuccessful endeavor with extraordinary personal and societal consequences.

Even "successful" marriages may only be defined as successful because they've lasted. My hope is to try to be at least somewhat instructive in describing significant differences between men and women and what the expectations and needs both sexes have for meaningful relationships and specifically for marriages.

Is it possible to be at least somewhat "scientific" in selecting our mate or is it at least possible to apply some predictable behaviors to maintain a happy and satisfying long term relationship with a single individual? Much of what I will be discussing has to do with the initial attraction we have for certain people and specifically for the people we marry and how much of this attraction has to do with issues which seem to be unconscious. Why can't we be married to just anyone? Or can we? Why does our selection process seem to be so flawed? Or is it?

With so much "on the line," it would seem only reasonable that there would be considerable education and training required before marriage would be considered or allowed. In fact, the only "requirement" in most states is for both people to be over the age of 18 and to have $20.00 in their pockets. Is there any other "career" decision with such minimal criteria?

I've had many people read this document as I've worked on it over the years. A frequently asked question is why I wrote it in the first place. As is true for many things we do in our lives, it has to do with personal experiences and the questions that arise about life as we "live and learn." Our society has changed dramatically during my lifetime. One of the major changes has involved relationships and marriages. There were "rules" when I was growing up and now there seem to be none or at least very few when it comes to male/female involvement. The frequency of divorce appears to be at an all time high and the number of single parent families and "blended" families is enormous. There continues to be a strong need for people to be in "relationships" but they rarely, if ever, have the expected or anticipated outcome.

There have already been many books written about this subject and I've been told that everything you are about to read has already been written. That may well be the case but I've never seen it done quite this way. I include many personal experiences because it's these experiences that are the basis for the "assumptions" I make in the book. Much of what I write may not apply to the younger generations. Most of the people I've questioned are over the age of 40. Also, it may not apply to people from different cultures.

Personal background

I've been married and divorced twice. I have two children from my first marriage and I've watched them struggle with the consequences of the marital disruptions. I've watched many others going through the same thing. Also, I'm a physician. I've been in the practice of Internal Medicine for 40 years and, as a physician, I've wondered if there isn't something that can be done to prevent all of this pain and suffering.

Basic assumptions

Before I get into the body of the work, I need to explain two of my thought processes. My first assumption is that all people are born basically "good." We may be upset by certain behaviors, but there are very few people out there who intend to hurt us or make our lives miserable.

My second assumption is that if something doesn't make sense, it's because you don't have all the facts. Early in my medical life, I would experience things that made "no sense." My response to these events was usually to just think "that's nuts." Then I would dismiss it as such and move on. Over the years, I've learned things that have "filled in the blanks." With the blanks filled in, these events that were "nuts" made perfect sense.

So, now, if something doesn't make sense, I look for all possible explanations which might "fill in the blanks." I've decided that people don't do things for "no reason." If a person responds in a certain way to something—it isn't "nuts." Sometimes these "fill in the blank" delays can be long. On one recent occasion, it took about 30 years! But, once I had the "data," 30 years of behavior made "perfect sense."

Identical versus unique

Also, before I proceed, I need to present my main premise. All people are unique. Everyone realizes this fairly early in life. If, for no other reason, people realize that their appearance is different from other people. The obvious exception to this is people who are identical twins or even identical triplets. Even these individuals realize that being "identical" is very "unique."

It is not my intent to address the things that make us all "unique." It is my intent to focus on those things that make us all "identical." My assumption is, that in most respects, we are "identical."

This means that when I'm happy, I feel just like you do when you're happy. The same applies to when I'm sad, angry, discouraged, tired, in pain, and so on. If something applies to me it applies to everyone!! Now, obviously, this is not always the case. Everyone reading this will disagree with some of the observations I'm making as they apply to them as individuals. It's never possible to be 100% inclusive with anything. I do feel, however, that most people will find that much of what I say does apply to them at least at some level.

As a physician, if we weren't all the same, I couldn't do my job. Not only does this apply to symptoms for various diseases, it applies to feelings. When people first come into my office, I have a pretty good idea of how they're feeling before I even ask them a question. I can tell if they're relaxed, tense, frightened, angry, in pain etc. This is because everyone's body language is basically the same.

People who are depressed look "depressed," talk "depressed," walk "depressed," and sit "depressed." The same applies for other emotional and physically feelings.

Can you tell how your kids are doing in the morning before you talk to them? Your spouse? Your boss? The people you see walking down the street? People you see in movies or TV? I would argue that you can because you are also aware of the common body language characteristics.

Innate versus Learned

I would argue that these characteristics are innate as opposed to learned. We are "hard wired" to behave this way and it isn't really something we can control. If a patient comes into my office and appears depressed, I will ask about their mood. Quite often, they will indicate that they are "fine" and certainly not depressed. In those situations, I will always rely on their body language to define their true mood.

It's not something we can hide.

Perception

Have you ever entered a room filled with people you didn't know and felt instantly uncomfortable? Why do we feel that way? I usually look around to try to find the reason for my discomfort and find no obvious cause. Also, I feel instantly better when I leave!

There are times when I've observed people, even from behind, and feel uncomfortable. What am I responding to? There are, also, many times when I meet someone for the first time and feel instantly at ease. What am I responding to? Presumably, these situations involve body language at some subtle levels. Something is either very right or very wrong. There are songs and stories about people who see other people across a room and there is instant attraction. I know a man who met his wife "across a room." He saw her and had this instant unbelievable attraction. He didn't even meet or talk to her at that time but met her several days later purely by chance. They are now married with three children.

We all have friends. Why are some people our friends and others aren't? Why are we comfortable around some people and not others? I don't have answers for this. I just know it's the way it is.

Men and Women Discussing Each Other

Men and women are very different in many ways. We typically have very little understanding of each other. With this in mind, I should probably qualify my assumption that I am just like all people to only include men. I would argue that the only thing dumber than two men discussing women is three men discussing women and vice-versa. For the record, the observations about women in this work come from women, not men. Keep in mind that I'm a typical man and have no more of an understanding of women than other men.

The Family Unit

Also, I will touch on the seeming importance of the integrity of a family unit and specifically parent–child/children interactions. This is because it's my assumption that it's easier for children to develop into happy and stable adults if they have both a mother and a father and if their parents live together.

The Research

My "research" has basically involved asking many people the same questions. These people include patients, friends, relatives and total strangers. As a physician, my job involves asking questions. Over the years, I've developed ways of obtaining information through questioning. Although, many of the questions are somewhat personal, most people are very willing to talk about themselves if they feel comfortable and the questions are presented in a non-threatening manner. From a purely legal standpoint, some of the questions would be considered "leading" if they were submitted in a court of law. I was operating with an agenda. Still, the consistency of the responses was virtually always there and most people really seemed to enjoy discussing the topics.

Chapter 2

What Makes Us "Tick"?

Our Genes and /or Our Environment

WE ARE THE product, or victims, of our genes and our environment. The personality impact of "nature" versus "nurture" has been discussed and debated for hundreds if not thousands of years and this has been the topic of many books. The intent of this work is to primarily look at the issue of "nature." I am assuming that "nature" is essentially established at birth and doesn't change. It's based on our genetic makeup. Obviously, a lot of how we function is affected by our environment and how we're raised. I certainly don't mean to minimize this. It's just that it is unique to each person and, thereby, makes generalizing virtually impossible. I intend to generalize a lot in this work.

Why Bring This Up?

My purpose in discussing this is to point out that there are clearly differences between men and women and these differences have presumably been critical in the survival of the species.

What determines our genetic make-up? Most everyone realizes that we get two sets of genes at the time of conception. One set from our "father" and one set from our "mother." Our parents got their genes from their "parents" who got their genes from their "parents" who got their genes from their "parents" and so forth. One of the major genetic characteristics is sexual determination. We are either male or female.

Thousands of years ago, our relatives survived because they functioned in ways that allowed them to survive. Although I doubt there is any way to know for sure, I assume that there was some type of a family unit consisting of a man, a woman and children.

Survival of The Fittest

The environment in which they lived was presumably quite hostile. There were great risks to life and limb on a daily basis. The men presumably did the hunting. I can imagine a group of men hunting a mastodon or some other large, dangerous animal. Assuming that they were successful, each man would have had a share of the kill.

A man could take his share off by himself and eat it, or he could brave mountains, streams and other dangers to take it back to his "family." If this assumption is accurate, it's obvious which "gene pool" would be "passed on." If he was killed, the only way the "family" could survive would be for them to be cared for by the community or by another man. If any of this is accurate, it would require that there be certain genetic characteristics that would determine how men and woman behave and react. There would be some innate differences. There would be some "hard wiring" that's taken place over the eons.

Chapter 3

Personalities

Psychiatrists and Psychologists

EVERYONE HAS A "personality." Certain personality characteristics seem to be established by our genes. When you watch new born babies in a nursery, they each seem to have a different "personality." Some sleep more than others, some cry more, some respond differently to being held. Even baby boys seem to be different than baby girls and there is now new research which may account for this.

How soon are we "hard wired" and stuck with "who we are" and how much can we change? Even personality characteristics that may not be "hard wired" from birth appear to be "hard wired" soon after birth. Perhaps even by age two or three. Psychiatrists and psychologists test for and define and classify personalities. There are a number of tests which are used to this end. There are many personality types. People with certain personality types can be challenging and even dangerous. It's usually best to avoid relationships with these individuals. Unfortunately, recognizing them can be virtually impossible without professional skills.

The Minnesota Multiphasic

A number of years ago, I had weekly dinners with a clinical psychologist—an extremely bright man with a very eclectic and interesting practice. He was an expert in a test called the MMPI-Minnesota Multiphasic Personality Inventory. One of the ironies of this was the fact that this test was developed in Minnesota where I was born and raised and one of the developers of the test was Dr. Starke Hathaway who lived in the same apartment building as my parents when they were first married.

My classmates and I took this test a number of times as we went through school. I assume this was done, at least partly, to determine the "questions" and the "answers." Also, when I went to the University of Minnesota Medical School, it was a test you had to "pass" to be admitted. It's a very strange test, if you've never taken it, and you wonder how anyone can make any sense out of it at all. There is even a scale which indicates whether you are trying to "fool" the test which is really interesting because I'm not sure how you could fool the test even if you tried. At any rate, the argument is that the test will be the same throughout your life. Your personality is set early on and can't be changed.

I distinctly remember one night when this psychologist came into the restaurant with a big smile on his face. He had "changed" someone's MMPI for the first time ever and was absolutely thrilled. Unfortunately, the next week he was very discouraged because when he re-examined the test he realized that he had miss-scored it and there had been no "personality change."

On another occasion we were discussing marriage counseling. He was conflicted professionally while working with a certain couple because he had given them both the MMPI which he did with all his clients. Based on their MMPIs, he felt they were not at all well suited for each other and should probably have never gotten married in the first place.

He would also counsel men going through their mid-life crises. Again, he would give them the MMPI, and more often than not would determine that, even though they might have been extraordinarily successful professionally, the careers they had chosen were a big mistake based on their personalities. They were now finally doing the things they really wanted to do or should have been doing all along. I mention this because I will be commenting on it later.

Different planets

There is a book that has been around for a number of years written by John Gray called "Men are from Mars, Women are from Venus." It basically discusses "differences between men and women." It certainly has some interesting observations. If I'd read it before I did, I might have saved myself a lot of grief. But, not reading it, added some different experiences to my life. The only suggestion I might make to the theories in the book is, that not only are men and women from different planets but different languages are spoken on those planets. The words and sentence structure are identical but the languages are still very different and there don't appear to be any dictionaries or translators.

I think this is a book that is well worth reading for both men and women. It discusses many of the behaviors that distinguish men and woman. The goal is to help us have a realization that men and women behave in consistent and even predicable ways and that these ways are "sex specific." I'm not going to do a review of the entire book but I am going to comment on one of his observations. This is for the benefit of those of you who haven't read the book and because it applies to our everyday interactions.

When women complain, what do they want? When men complain what do they want?

Answers: When women complain, they want someone to listen. They, typically, aren't interested in a solution or even suggestions. They don't want them! When men complain, they want a solution or at least advice if the listener has any. They don't want someone to "just listen." This may be because men appear to be "solvers." From a man's standpoint, it's hard to listen to a "problem" and not try to help.

From a professional standpoint, this can become a real challenge. Women patients are coming in with "complaints" and I always assume they are there for solutions if I have any. To just listen and not offer any advice seems totally counterintuitive. I can't imagine that saying "I'm sorry you're so upset" and then getting up and leaving the exam room would be appropriate.

This doesn't apply, however, to the complaints I hear from women I see in a non-professional environment. In those settings, women don't necessarily want my advice. I have to really concentrate so that I "just listen." I have yet to figure out when women really want my suggestions in a non-professional setting. Perhaps never!

For the women reading this, if a man is complaining he's looking for advice or help. Just listening and being sympathetic isn't what we're after.

Different Brains, Oh Well

In many other areas, men's and women's brains appear to function in somewhat different ways. Many times, when I'm having a conversation with a woman, she will say something "off the wall." At least it seems "off the wall" to me. When I've commented that I don't understand why she said what she said, she can always explain it. When she explains it, I can see how she got there. It makes "perfect sense." I just would never have gotten there on my own. My brain simply doesn't work that way.

My mother used to do this. My family consisted of four people. My mother and father and a brother who is 17 months older. We would be having a conversation at mealtime and our mother would suddenly say something "off the wall." My brother and I would glance at each other and then at our dad. He would be biting his lip to keep from laughing. One of us would then start to choke to keep from laughing and have to leave the table. When things finally settled down, the one who left the table would return. At that point, my mother would ask, "Is there something wrong with the food?" At which point, the whole process would recur. It never seemed to fail! Keep in mind that sitting at the table were three male brains and one female brain. I suspect things would have been different if my parents had had a son and a daughter or two daughters rather than two sons. My mother was a very bright woman. She always had a reason for what she said when she said it. Our brains were just on a different frequency-or something. For those old enough to remember, this was the basis for the George Burns and Gracie Allen comedy series.

What this means is that women aren't really "illogical." Their "logic" is just different than "male logic." I'm not sure this can be or needs to be "fixed." It's actually quite fascinating. I would hope that just realizing we speak different languages and, that our translations may be incorrect, might be enough to avoid at least some of the wrong assumptions.

Tearing Up

When it comes to emotions, women are typically viewed as the "weaker" sex. Over the years, this has not been my experience. There are clearly some socially accepted differences regarding emotional expression. Women are given far greater latitude than men. This is certainly true when it comes to crying.

Women appear to "tear up" for a number of reasons. They do it when they're happy, sad, angry, frightened, in pain, when they're trying to get out of doing something, when they want something and when their hormones are in flux.

Men seem to only "tear up" when they're sad or at least emotionally impacted. They don't tend to do it when they're happy, angry, frightened or in pain.

Personally, I "tear up" a lot. I suspect more than many women. All men do. We just don't like to be seen crying so you may never have actually seen a man cry. We prefer to do it in private. If a man cries when I'm seeing him professionally, I know that something is really wrong.

I've gone to a number of funerals over the years. I've occasionally been asked to stand up and make some comments. This has never gone well. I invariably "break down." Also, looking around the church, I've noticed that it's typically the men who are having trouble "keeping it together." Women are much better at this than men.

When our parents died, my brother and I both wanted to make some comments. The only way we were able to accomplish this was by recording our eulogies and then playing them on a tape recorder. It would have been a real struggle for us both if we'd tried to stand up and talk.

Loss of a Loved One

Women, also, seem to handle the loss of a loved one better than men. It's my professional opinion that when it comes to dying, the man should always die first. It's not that wives, necessarily, do well after the loss of a spouse- they just seem to do better than husbands.

The "prevailing wisdom," after the loss of a loved one, suggests that you should be emotionally better after one year and "normal" after two. I don't think this applies to either sex, but for men it seems to take years before they are emotionally stable again.

The "magic" number seems to be eight years. Although not necessarily "good news," hearing this can be very reassuring to a man who is six years out from the loss of the woman he loved and still struggling. At least he's not abnormal. This time frame may, also, apply to women. It doesn't come up as often with them as it does with men because they're less likely to break down when their deceased husband comes into the conversation years after his death.

Because of this, I've decided that women are much more resilient than men when it comes to emotional stability. They may cry but that doesn't mean they aren't "tough."

"Prevailing Wisdom"

My recent professional life involved taking care of many people in a retirement home setting. My office was physically in a retirement home and, because of that, many of my patients lived there. Before I moved my office into that location, I had certain pre-conceived ideas about who took care of whom in a marriage. The "prevailing wisdom." This was based on what are perceived to be the traditional male/female roles. What I learned was that my pre-conceived ideas were, frequently, wrong. My nurse of over 30 years, made the same observation.

It turns out, that, at least in this facility, if the husband became sick or disabled, the wife often turned to the facility to provide his care. If the wife, on the other hand, became sick or disabled the husband frequently provided the "lion's share" of the support and care—even to the point of compromising his own health. It happened repeatedly. This even occurred with my parents who lived at the retirement home. Part of this, obviously, has to do with physical strength. But that didn't appear to be the only explanation. Because of that experience, I have looked for similar examples away from the retirement home and the same behavior seems to prevail.

A possible explanation would be based on my theories of how we got here. If they are accurate at any level, men would need to be "hard wired" to do everything possible to keep the woman they "love" alive and well. Losing her would be devastating to him as well as to the family unit.

Women, on the other hand, would have needed to be able to "move on" if their husbands died. If they couldn't, the survival of the children would be at risk as would that gene pool. This may well be overly simplistic, but it could also "explain" why women's "love" may be different than men's. Women would need to be more "pragmatic."

Chapter 4

Sexual Attraction &
Sexual Behavior

No X-Rating Intended

IT WASN'T AND isn't my intent to make this an x-rated book. As a physician, I'm expected to be able to answer questions from both men and women about how their bodies work. I'm capable of doing this for most things because men and women are basically the same. When it comes to intimate matters, however, I know relatively little about how women's minds or bodies work. This was not a subject that was stressed in medical school in the 1960's. The following information about women has come from conversations I've had with women I've known over the years. It hasn't come from any books I've read. Some of this information could probably be considered x-rated. So, read on at your own risk.

All animals, including humans, are sexual creatures. The attraction for men and women is clearly sexual. It has always been assumed that men, after puberty, have "raging hormones" and that this is a uniquely male characteristic. What I've learned through conversations with women is that they can also have "raging hormones" and that a sexual relationship is extremely important.

Of interest is the fact that a given man is not attracted to all women and vice versa. What is it that attracts us only to certain members of the opposite sex? I'm aware of no one having the answer to this question. I haven't even heard any good theories.

Orgasm or Not

For women, as well as men, having an orgasm during sexual relations is important, although, apparently not essential. Some women, with whom I've visited, have never had an orgasm during intercourse and actually believe that it isn't even possible. For a woman, having an orgasm apparently requires more than just physical stimulation. It also requires that her brain be actively involved. Indeed, for women, the brain may be the most "erotic" organ. If she feels loved and safe it makes a huge difference. Also, women can have multiple orgasms while a man is only having one. They can have a very short "reset" time. This is not, typically, the case for men.

Apparently, what really matters to many women is being held and kissed not necessarily having an orgasm. I have no argument with that. But, if that's the case, see to it that the man who loves you understands that.

Women who don't have orgasms will, on occasion, act as if they have. Reasons I've been given to explain this have included:

1) "To get it over with" or
2) To allow him to "feel like a man."

They apparently assume that men are selfish creatures who are simply interested in "being satisfied" and are less interested in what's happening with the women they're with.

Well, men do care. They care a lot. If, for no other reason, there has to be parity. No man wants to owe anybody anything.

We need to feel that things are "fair." If we don't, we're not content. This, also, applies to "making love." If a woman is "lying" to the man who loves her, she is doing them both a great disservice.

For what it's worth, there are a number of ways for a woman to "climax." If the man loves you, he will do "what it takes." This, however, requires tremendous trust. Both people have to feel safe. They have to be willing to talk about a very "delicate" subject. Also, it needs to be remembered that the most erogenous organ in a woman's body is her brain.

Erection or Not

From a pure stimulation standpoint, it is mandatory that a man maintain an erection long enough. If he doesn't, it may be because he has what is referred to as "premature ejaculation." This is a common problem especially in young men, but it can persist throughout one's life. We now have medications which can treat this. Previously, the treatment for this was, at best, difficult.

Also, throughout life, men of all ages can have trouble achieving and maintaining an erection. If a man is afraid he won't be able to achieve an erection, he won't. If he has an erection and is afraid he might "lose it," he will. The brain, it turns out, is an extraordinarily powerful organ when it comes to intimacy for men as well as women. There are a number of reasons that men can't achieve or maintain an erection. The brain is only one of them. Fortunately, we now have a number of ways of helping men with these problems.

It turns out that when men can't achieve or maintain an erection, women frequently blame themselves! They aren't attractive enough or "sexy" enough! They feel inadequate! This can have a profound effect on their self image. This is truly unfortunate because it typically is not the issue. Again, this is clearly a very sensitive topic and I suspect very few couples ever really discuss their sexual needs and what it takes to have those needs met. They are only making assumptions and these assumptions are frequently incorrect.

It is my assumption that most men and women ultimately want a stable and enjoyable monogamous long term relationship. They don't want to be constantly "playing the field." Variety is not necessarily the "spice of life." The problem seems to be that stable and enjoyable monogamous relationships are not common as they should be. It, also, appears that everyone assumes that the only reason for not having a stable and enjoyable monogamous relationship is a selection process. One just needs to find the right person and that person is probably just around the corner. Typically, people leave one relationship and immediately start looking for another. I know of a woman who has been married 23 times presumable trying to find "Mr. Right"! Something just isn't working!

The Road Ahead–The Questions To Be Answered

The balance of the book is, therefore, going to try to answer the following questions:

1. How do women think and what do they want and expect from a relationship?
2. How do men think and what do the want and expect from a relationship?
3. Why are so many relationships and marriages "not working" and is there anything that can be done to change this?

Chapter 5

Assumptions & Behavior

Making Assumptions; Right and Wrong

It's always been assumed that men's and women's brains function in different ways. We now have technology that allows us to actually see what is happening in our brains in real time. What we're learning from these studies confirms what has always been assumed. As time goes by, our knowledge level will probably rapidly increase.

One characteristic which seems to be present in the ways that both men and women process information is our willingness and need to make assumptions. Everyone makes assumptions. I've made assumptions with this work. We make assumptions constantly throughout every day of our life. When we approach an intersection and the light for us is green, we assume that the people coming on the cross street will stop since their light will presumably be red and they will know what red means. We assume that the food we buy is safe to eat and that the banks are taking care of the money we've deposited with them.

Projection

A big part of making assumptions has to do with a psychological term called "projection." "Projection" means that you assign your feelings and attitudes to others. You assume that everyone thinks and acts just like you do for the same reasons. In other words, we're all alike!

Assumptions are frequently negative. If there are two or even three possible explanations for a certain comment or a certain behavior, we frequently assume the one that is the most destructive in it's outcome. This, also, applies to medicine. When people experience a symptom, they fear the worst. They almost always have something in mind as to the diagnosis and it's usually negative. This is especially true for older patients. This is understandable because they know they're on the "down slope" of life.

Still, much of my day is spent simply reassuring people that they aren't going to die, at least not that day, from the heart disease or cancer they don't have. One of the most common and reassuring comments I make to my patients as they leave the exam room is "you're fixable." This, they understand and remember.

Wrong Assumptions; Incorrect Decisions

I would now argue that wrong assumptions are the basis for a great deal of unhappiness in, and for the breaking up of, many relationships and marriages with all the attending consequences.

When two people are interacting and one responds to something said or done by making a wrong assumption and behaves accordingly, the other person won't understand the response, and, can then make a similar wrong assumption and act accordingly. This can obviously have extraordinarily negative consequences.

This is particularly important when it comes to men and women because, as will be discussed, we process information so differently and come to very different conclusions about many situations in our lives. When I discuss "how men think" with women, they are usually amazed and typically argue with me at length. They can't believe that there is such a difference.

Chapter 6

Men

Simplicity

MEN ARE FREQUENTLY described as "simple." This means that if a man wants something, he asks for it or if he says something he means just that. There's no ambiguity. Woman, on the other hand, are much more complicated. This will be addressed in greater length at the end of this chapter.

If you ask a woman, at least an older woman, why men marry you will typically get one of two reasons and quite often both. The answers are:

1) "To be taken care of" and , usually after a pause,
2) "For sex ."

The reason I mention "older women" is that there appears to be a generational difference as far as this is concerned. Younger women don't necessarily give these answers but they, also, don't argue with them if they are "offered" as choices.

To Be Taken Care Of

As far as the first answer is concerned, I would argue that men not only don't need to, but don't really want to be "taken care of." Personally, I'm currently single. I don't have the neatest house in the world, I'm not the best cook and my clothes aren't always ironed. My house, however, is "neat enough" for me, I'm not starving and my clothes may not always be ironed but they are clean.

Just to keep the record straight, I'm very capable of keeping my house "spotless," I do actually cook, and not only do I know how to wash and iron clothes, I can also sew, darn socks, knit and crochet. Even if I couldn't, I can well afford to hire someone to do these things for me. I don't need to be married to have these services provided. That's not to say that it isn't nice to have someone provide a clean house, clean clothes and food on the table. It just isn't one of the reasons men marry.

Sex, of Course

What about sex? If all a man is interested in is sex, he certainly doesn't need to get married to have this need met. In this regard, it's necessary to keep in mind that there is a difference between "having sex" and "making love." I'm not sure if women realize that for men there is a clear distinction.

The "prevailing wisdom" for women appears to be that men are "driven" by sex and that they are perfectly content having sex frequently and with almost anyone. They also appear to think that this applies to married as well as single men and that it's not only accepted behavior among men but men envy other men who seem to have multiple "conquests" on an ongoing basis. They assume that this is "normal" male behavior and that most single men really enjoy "playing the field" and most married men are "unfaithful."

Common Knowledge

When I ask them how they know this, they essentially say that it's "common knowledge." Now it may be "common knowledge" but I know a lot of men and, although this is not a frequent topic of conversation, I don't know any who "play around" on their wives and, if they did, it would be a cause for disrespect not envy. Personally, I never had any inclination to be "unfaithful" when I was married and I suspect the same applies to virtually all married men. For what it's worth, losing the respect of your peers is about the worst thing that can happen to a man. We need to feel that our friends and associates respect us.

Sex and Making Love

People can have "sex" in many places and with many people. "Making love" is a whole different matter. Men express their love in ways that women frequently don't understand or sense. Men express their love by working hard and being good providers. By making sure they live in a safe environment. By making sure the car works. By making sure the lawn is mowed. By making sure that their wives and family will be cared for if something happens to them. These don't necessarily qualify as romantic traits but without them, I would argue, life could be very complicated. For a man, "making love" is a special way of "showing love." Men assume the person they love wants to "make love" as well. Why wouldn't they? It's an extraordinary way to show love. It's frequently all a man needs! Not "having sex" but "making love."

Mistresses

Obviously, some men do have mistresses. Why is that? I can only assume, because I haven't done the "research." Maybe some men like "variety." Maybe, it's an issue of insecurity and it's a way to prove they're still attractive and "sexy." Still "macho." Maybe, however, it's because the woman they love is no longer interested in "making love." Maybe because she doesn't feel loved.

If this is the case and it's a choice of "sex or no sex" most men will choose "sex." This would account for the "world's oldest profession" and explain why men will have sex with women they don't love.

I'm convinced that most men would prefer to have the woman they love be the love in their life.

So, What is Love?

With this in mind, I would argue that, basically, men marry for one reason only and that's Love. So what's Love? Love is not something that I can define but I know what it is. Men and women appear to have different definitions for the terms "loving someone" and "being in love" with someone.

Men consider these terms synonymous whereas women make a clear distinction. At least this is true for romantic men-women relationships. A man will "love" his children and his parents and even special "friends" but those appear to be different feelings than what he feels for the woman he loves.

Also, men don't typically talk about loving a woman other than their wife. Women will talk about loving a number of men but that doesn't mean they are "in love" with those men. For them, "being in love" is a term reserved for a single man. If a man "loves" a woman it means that he is, also, "in love" with her. If a woman "loves" a man she isn't necessarily "in love" with him.

Love at First Sight

I've been in love four times in my life. Each time it was "slam dunk" and I still have strong emotional feelings for all the women I've loved even though those experiences have proven "challenging."

I didn't invent the term "love at first sight." I didn't write the song "He stopped loving her today!" I wasn't the first person to observe that "love is blind."

I just know that "love at first sight" applies to me and I also know it applies to many, if not all, men. Men are not anxious to acknowledge that they fell in love at first sight because it makes no sense. Even if they won't concede "love at first sight," they will almost always admit that "there was something special" happening right away. There was "chemistry." Also, they will usually admit that "chemistry" is rare. Most men haven't been "in love" many times in their lives. It doesn't happen with every woman who comes along.

Love and Marriage

Being in love doesn't always lead to marriage and some men have obviously married women they didn't love. Two occasions when men may marry when they aren't "in love" is if a pregnancy is involved or if, for some other reason, they would feel "guilty" if they didn't get married. I would suggest that those are occasions where marriage may not be the best course of action. If a man is not "in love" with his wife, I would expect things to be a real struggle.

Four Times in Love

How do I know I've only been in love four times? What about all the other women I've dated? What was the difference? The difference actually was apparent "after the fact." When the relationships with the "women I loved" ended, I was emotionally distraught. I had all the classical symptoms of depression and they lasted for a considerable period of time. When my other relationships ended, there was no such trauma. Quite often, it was almost a relief. The strange thing is that these other women have been bright, talented and wonderful people. It just wasn't "love at first sight" and I never "learned" to love any of these women if it wasn't there initially. I've never really been able to understand this but at least for me it's been "reality." If one assesses "arranged marriages," this, also, appears to be true for them. If love isn't there initially, it doesn't appear to develop with time.

Dating Leads To?

Will men date women they don't love? Will they sleep with them? Will they even live with them? The answer to each of these questions is yes. But, unless they love them, they probably won't marry them. That doesn't mean that they don't like them or enjoy being with them. It just means that, for men, love is a requirement for marriage.

Husband Love

It's been my experience that if you ask a woman if her husband loves her, she will quite often respond

"I think so" or "I hope so." If you ask a man if his wife loves him, he will usually respond "Huh?." For a man, it's assumed that his wife loves him. Why else would she have married him? For a woman, this appears to be less "clear cut."

Cute/Handsome

It's often said that men are visual—much more so than women. That may be true, but whenever I hear women talk about someone for the first time they usually include a physical description. Frequently they refer to someone as "cute" or "handsome" or "gorgeous" or terms that suggest the opposite. This applies to both men and women. I'm not sure I've ever heard a man describe the women in his life using any of those terms.

They might say something like "I just met the nicest lady" to a woman and she will ask "Is she cute?" Or a daughter will be describing her new "boyfriend" to her mother and say how "cute" he is. Or the mother will ask if he is "cute." Again, it's not that men don't care, but it isn't something we comment on much. At least, this seems to be true when it comes to our "significant other." Beauty clearly appears to be in the eyes of the beholder. Indeed, I've decided that the most important "beauty" is in the eyes. This is what seems to set people apart. This may have a lot to do with "love at first sight." Pardon the pun. Maybe, we "fall in love" with someone's eyes.

Now, several more men/women differences.

Teasing

The first has to do with teasing. Men tease people they like. We tease the people we really like the most. I'm constantly teasing my friends and they tease me. I'm sure psychologists will indicate that teasing can be a form of aggression. That's not the type of teasing I'm talking about. If my friends quit "teasing" me, I would worry. Because of this, it's hard for a man not to tease the women for whom he really cares.

Women frequently don't see it that way. If you see two women "teasing" each other they probably are really angry. To them "teasing" can be very hurtful. Men, therefore, need to be very careful about the things they say to women.

One of the major consequences of this is that men don't realize that the things we're saying and doing are causing pain. If we were "paying attention" we would notice that the woman we're teasing isn't appreciating what we're doing and we would apologize. Since we're oblivious, we see no reason to apologize. Apologize for what? So, here is a woman whose feelings have been really hurt and the man who did it doesn't apologize. What a cad!!! Here is a man who thinks everything is fine but, all of a sudden, he's in the "doghouse" and doesn't know why. So he asks and the response is "nothing." For the definition of "nothing" see below.

Eye Contact

The second difference has to do with eye contact during conversations .When women talk to each other, they maintain eye contact. At least when they are in serious conversation. When men talk to each other, they don't maintain eye contact. At least not for very long. Eye contact can imply competition or aggression. "Who blinks first?" What's the first rule of avoiding "road rage"? Don't make eye contact! The problem is,therefore, if a man isn't maintaining eye contact with a woman when they are having a conversation, she doesn't think he's listening. This can be very frustrating and irritating as far as a woman is concerned. Another dilemma!

Old Simple Me

The last and perhaps the most important difference has to do with the fact that men are "simple" and women are "complicated." If a man wants something, he asks, He asks for help, advice, and opinions along with more mundane things like what he wants to eat.

Women, on the other hand, expect men to anticipate their needs. In fact, if they have to ask, things get very complicated. If a man responds to a request after being asked, it doesn't seem to "count." It means that he's "insensitive." If he was "sensitive," he would have known what to say or do without being asked and "sensitivity" ranks high in women's lists of important attributes in a man.

Also, women will often say things they think the man wants to hear even if she doesn't really mean it. Men will always assume that what is said is what is meant. You can imagine where this can lead.

Chapter 7

Women

Security and Safety

IF MEN MARRY for "love" why, then, do women marry? It appears that women may marry for reasons other than "love." Frequently, I'm told, it's for security or because they want a family- the biological clock is ticking. Security, for a woman, appears to be one of the most important concepts in a relationship. Security also appears to be one of those words defined differently by men and women.

To women it means a number of things, but perhaps the most important is safety. For men, security appears to involve primarily financial issues. If a woman marries for security, in a man's eyes, it means that she wants someone who will be able to "support" her and the children. She's marrying for money.

For women, financial issues are not irrelevant, but security also means safety and trust. They need to know that they are in no physical or emotional danger and that their husbands are honest and will come home at night. Women appear to have an initial "attraction" to a man but there may not be "love at first sight."

"Love" for women seems to take time to develop. It may not even happen until after they are married and, apparently, sometimes it never happens. I've asked women who are divorced if they ever "loved" their husbands and they frequently say that they "thought" they loved them but then realized that they didn't. I've never heard a man say that. A man either loves the woman in his life or not.

Checklists

Also, women appear to have a "checklist." Even if they are very much attracted to a man he must, also, have characteristics that make him an "appropriate" mate. If he doesn't, they will "move on." I've even known women who were engaged but still dated and even married other men—presumably men with a better "list" of characteristics.

Men don't seem to have a "checklist"- at least not a list that "trumps" love. That's not to say that things other than "love" aren't important to men. It is to suggest that men "fall in love" first and then look at the other factors. These factors generally are far less important "after the fact."

With a possible "male checklist" in mind, women apparently feel that they can "catch" a man by acting in certain ways. I've known women who "pretend" to like sports, certain music, to travel or even a man's friends just to "catch him." Presumably, attempting to have as many of the "checks" as possible. Then, once he's "caught," she no longer needs to "play the game" and can just "be her self."

I would again like to emphasize that men's checklists don't work that way. They fall in love and then check the list. Not vice -versa. I know lots of women who like the things I like. Many of them are also very charming and attractive. I just don't love them and even though we might be very well matched, being around them doesn't seem to change that It just doesn't seem to work that way.

On Line

This may, again, be a generational issue. Many people now seem to be meeting "on line" and are being "matched up" based on interests. Although the ads suggest that this type of "match making" frequently leads to marriage, it doesn't ft very well with my theories. I would still assume that, at least for the man, there would need to be "love at first sight." This, also, applies to certain "match making" television shows.

It appears to me that the way women choose their future mates is far more practical than the way men do.

Expressing Love Now and Again

One of the most important and significant differences between men and women is the need to be told and shown that they're "loved." Women appear to need this almost daily. It's as if they need reassurance that they are really special. Men aren't necessarily very good at this. Perhaps, it's because they don't appear to need the same constant reassurance. They assume they're loved and special.

There is an old Norwegian story that goes something like this: Olga and Lars had been married for 50 years. They went out for dinner to celebrate. During the meal, Lars asked Olga if there was anything special she would like. Olga responded by asking him to tell her that he loved her. Lars responded by telling her that he told her he loved her 50 years ago when they got married, and that he would let her know if he ever changed his mind.

Unfortunately, there is a certain amount of truth to this story which is part of the reason that it's funny – at least for men. As an aside, even if Lars had said "I love you" when Olga asked, it wouldn't have "counted." Remember, if women have to ask for something, doing or saying it doesn't count. Men need to "read their minds."

To Be Touched and Held

Women, also, really like to be touched. This is another one of those characteristics that appears to distinguish women from men. When woman are talking with each other they are frequently touching each other as well. When women walk they are frequently holding arms. Perhaps this is why women are willing to have "one night stands" or "casual sex"—especially in the current world where the "downside" can be so devastating. From my "research" what women want more than anything is to be held. If you want to really "get a reaction" from a woman who doesn't have a man in her life, ask her if she "doesn't miss being held." They don't seem to necessarily miss the sex part so much. They miss being held.

My mother loved hugs. I hug both of my kids because in the current world "that's the thing to do." But, there is a difference. Men, at least in our society, don't hug. It's very strange for most American men to watch men from other societies hug and kiss each other. It doesn't mean we don't care for each other in America and it certainly doesn't mean that the men from other societies do. Men don't seem to need to be hugged to feel loved and cared for. Women do! This is another one of those situations where there are different needs.

Not only does this not need to be a source of conflict, it appears that men's and women's needs are complementary.

Women want to be held and men want someone to hold. It seems to be more an issue of timing. Women need to be held often and sometimes the only time men think about holding the women they love is in bed. Also, it is one of those situations where there may be some societal and generational differences. Still, it always gives me a warm feeling when I see an "elderly" couple walking along hand in hand.

Conversations

Apparently when women sit around and visit, men are a frequent topic of conversation and the things said are quite often not very complimentary even if the men happen to be husbands. Women apparently assume that men do the same. The reality is that men rarely, if ever, talk about women. At least they don't if they are married and I can't remember any husband saying negative things about his wife. If things are said about wives they always seem to be complimentary. This is another one of those instances where women find this hard to believe. Apparently, since they are frequently talking about men they assume men are frequently talking about men. "Projection" in action.

Women can talk for hours. It seems as if they can talk for hours every day with the same woman or women. I haven't actually listened in on their conversations but it's always intrigued me. Is there really that much to talk about? This will, also, be commented on more later.

Restroom Visits

If women are in a social gathering and one needs to use the restroom, it seems to trigger some type of reflex in all the other women and they all head off. Have you ever seen men do this?

I've asked women about this and have yet to get a satisfactory answer. Apparently, there is not a lot of socializing going on while they are in the restroom. It's just something they do.

Different Memories

Men and women, also, seem to remember things differently. In fact, what I've also learned over the years, is that women seemingly remember every slight or hurtful thing that has ever happened to them. They seem to even remember the day and sometimes the hour! This doesn't seem to be true for men. We may remember something globally but not specifics. Also, the things that women find the most hurtful are things that never seem to bother men at all. That may be why they "don't remember." My daughter remembers many "hurtful" things that occurred when she was a teenager. I can't remember any of them, but she is extremely bright and her memory for the "good" things that occurred is just as good as for the "bad" things. This is another one of those things that can create conflict in relationships.

I've been in social situations with the same couples and the wife will bring up the same unpleasant memory repeatedly. The "poor" husband doesn't know what to do or what to say and I'm no help. I wonder if the wife is looking for some type of apology and would then quit raising the issue. More "research" is needed.

Common Knowledge

The following section was sent to me by email by a woman so I don't know who I should credit but it may fall in the category of "common knowledge."

Nine words women use:

1) Fine: This is a word women use to end an argument when they are right and you need to shut up.

2) Five Minutes: If she is getting dressed, this means half an hour. Five minutes is only five minutes if you have just been given five more minutes to watch the game before helping around the house.

3) Nothing: This is the calm before the storm. This means something and you should be on your toes. Arguments that begin with "nothing" usually end in "fine."

4) Go Ahead: This is a dare, not permission. Don't do it!

5) Loud Sigh: This is actually a word, but is a non-verbal statement often misunderstood by men. A loud sigh means she thinks you are an idiot and wonders why she is wasting her time standing here and arguing with you about nothing.{Refer back to #3 for the meaning of nothing}.

6) That's Okay: This is one of the most dangerous statements a woman can make to a man. That's okay means she wants to think long and hard before deciding how and when you will pay for your mistake.

7) **Thanks**: A woman is thanking you. Do not question or faint... Just say "you're welcome." If she says "Thanks a lot"—that is pure sarcasm and she is not thanking you at all. **Do Not** say "You're welcome" That will bring on a "Whatever."

8) **Whatever**: Is a woman's way of saying *Go To Hell.*

9) **Don't worry about it, I got it**: Another dangerous statement meaning this is something that a woman has told a man to do several times but is now doing it herself. This will later result in a man asking "what's wrong?" For the woman's response refer to #3.

The Ring

The last example I will give regarding women has to do with a couple I've known for years. Shortly after they met and started dating, he asked her to marry him and she said yes. Nothing further was said for nine months and no ring was forthcoming. Because of that, she thought he wasn't really serious and started dating someone else. No further discussion and no ring meant no contract from her standpoint. After nine months, he told her that the next Saturday they were gong to go to the jewelers. She asked why? He told her because they needed to pick out rings. She was totally surprised!

I've discussed this with many women and they agree with the woman.

I've discussed this with many men and they agree with the man.

Chapter 8

Relationships & Assumptions

Old Marriage

TRADITIONALLY, RELATIONSHIPS ENDED in marriage. Couples dated and then got married and began living together. Marriage usually occurred fairly early in life. There wasn't necessarily even a lot of dating. Couples would "fall in love" in high school or even grade school and then get married in their late teens or early twenties. It was rare to find someone unmarried after their mid-twenties. There was occasionally some "marriage counseling" done but this didn't usually happen until after people were already engaged and it was done by the minister, or priest or rabbi just before the marriage. People "in love" give very little thought to any potential "downside" and are not necessarily anxious or willing to listen to "advice" at this point in their lives. This is particularly true if the discussion suggests that the planned marriage should possible be "reconsidered."

Perfectly good relationships

In today's world, at least in our society, things are very different. Couples frequently are waiting longer before they actually marry and may even live together before any "long term" decisions are even discussed. They are even intentionally having children with no thoughts of marriage. The argument is that this allows couples to learn a lot about themselves as well as their "significant other" and that this will result in happier relationships and fewer divorces. On the surface, this does make sense but it doesn't appear to be substantiated by the actual statistics. It appears that just as many of these relationships fall apart after marriage. It's almost as if marriage messes up perfectly good relationships!

One can always argue that this is an issue of experience and maturity but this isn't always the case. I cared for an elderly couple a number of years ago who had both experienced marriage and divorce and decided that they had had enough of that. Because of this, they decided that they would just "live together." They did this for four years and were extremely happy. They were so happy, in fact, that they decided to get married after all. Four months later they were divorced and bitter beyond belief. They each accused the other of "changing" after the marriage. At least there weren't any kids involved!

Incorrect Assumptions

Based on my "research," relationships frequently begin with what appear to be incorrect assumptions.

As was indicated earlier, woman appear to marry primarily for safety and security and assume that men marry for sex and to be taken care of. For women to feel safe and secure, they need to feel loved.

From a woman's standpoint it doesn't take much to show her that she is loved. The words " I love you" everyday, hugs and kisses when you're not in bed, flowers at times other than birthdays and anniversaries, listening and not "solving," looking at her when you're talking, not teasing and apologizing when you've said or done something hurtful. Without these, she may, understandably, feel unloved.

Also, since men only marry for love, they assume their wives, also, only marry for love.

From a man's standpoint, it doesn't take much to show him that he is loved. It just requires physical responsiveness. Without that, he may, understandably, feel unloved.

Feeling Loved

So, if a woman doesn't feel loved, and believes that her husband only want his clothes washed, his meals on time and to have sex, how anxious is she going to be to wash his clothes, cook his meals and go to bed with him even if he is a good provider and doesn't beat her From a man's standpoint, the best way to show love is to "make love." Not have sex but "make love."

The unfortunate potential effect of this is to have two people who do love each other both feeling unloved and unappreciated.

Love and Respect

I'm not a theologian, but apparently the Bible says that men are to "love" their wives and women are to "respect" their husbands. I don't think that any relationship is going to be successful unless both parties love and respect each other but it's also possible that this is the basis for how men and women function. If nothing else, this is certainly consistent with men "falling in love" and women needing to make sure that their husbands have characteristics they can respect. Still, this implies that men rank higher than woman in the societal hierarchy.

Over the years, I have often heard women say, when they're asked what they do, that they're "only a housewife." My mother was "only a housewife" and if asked that's probably the answer she would have given. My mother never worked away from home but she was always working. In many ways, she worked harder than my dad.

I would argue that women who stay at home and take care of their families do the most important work that can be done. From the standpoint of societal survival, there is nothing more important than taking care of the children. This is clearly a task that can be left to others but I think that mothers do it better than anyone. I know no man who doesn't have extraordinary respect for women who are housewives.

It troubles me to think that many women seem to feel that unless they are in the workforce they don't have that much value. Certainly, women should be able to have careers outside of the home and they are obviously very capable of having them. In today's world, that almost seems like the norm. If, for no other reason, because of financial needs. If women are looking for respect from men, however, that isn't necessary.

Chapter 9

Communication

What's This?

THE MOST IMPORTANT aspect of any relationship is "communication." This is the word that comes up most often when women are talking about their frustration with the men in their lives. There is never enough "communication" between men and women as far as women are concerned. This is not a word you will hear coming out of a man's mouth very often. Men don't seem to have problems "communicating" with other men and don't realize how much trouble they're having "communicating" with the women in their lives. They're oblivious!

Saying What You Mean?

When men say something, that's what they mean. There are rarely hidden meanings unless perhaps you're visiting with a politician. Women, on the other hand, don't necessarily mean exactly what they're saying or at least they feel free to "change their minds."

Intuition

Women, also, seem to be much more intuitive when it comes to what other people are feeling. They seem to be more likely to respond to subtle messages and act accordingly. They have a "sixth sense" that men don't seem to have.

Women, from a man's standpoint, expect us to "read their minds." This isn't how men's minds seem to work. Remember if a woman has to ask for something, saying or doing it doesn't count. On the other hand, if a man wants something done, he asks. How else is someone to know?

Is Talking the Same as Communicating?

Women, for the most part, seem to be better "talkers" than men. They can sit for hours and just "visit." Most men talk for a reason. They have something in mind. Quite often it is solving a problem. If there's no problem to solve why waste your breath?

I continue to have weekly dinners with men. "Boy's Night Out." We typically visit for about an hour and then we're through and head home. I recently visited with one of the wives and she was amazed and puzzled by the fact that we "finished so fast." I hadn't really thought much about that until she mentioned it, but that's all we had to talk about. We were able to discuss the things that needed discussing that week in an hour. Makes sense to me!

Same Words, Same Language, But...

How do you communicate with someone who speaks a different language even though it sounds the same and it uses the same words and same sentence structure? This appears to be the dilemma with men and women.

How would you communicate with someone if you were dropped into a country where you don't speak the language and no one in the country speaks English? How would you get your needs met?

Most of us would rely on some type of sign language including body language and this would certainly work for a lot of things. We could indicate if we were hungry, sleepy, cold, hot, lost, in pain etc. and would almost certainly be understood. There could be a primitive level of "communication."

In some ways, the latter situation would almost be easier because you would at least realize that communication would be a real struggle. With men and women, we don't realize how complicated things really are.

It Doesn't Improve With Age

In my current medical practice, I've ended up assuming that what I say to a patient isn't being understood! I take care of a lot of elderly patients and their brains aren't always working very well and many of them can't hear. Many times both husbands and wives will be in the exam room to have two sets of ears and two brains to rely on. They will discuss symptoms and medications and frequently these conversations can be hilarious. The wife will say something which the husband mis-hears and he will respond to what he thought he heard. The wife will be totally confused and probably doesn't hear exactly what he said anyway. Pretty soon it's chaos.

After discussing my recommendations with them, I will always ask them what they thought I said and it's rare if they get it correct. I will then write things down and hope they don't lose the paper on the way to their car. Frequently, I will call the next day to see how they are doing and hope that they can hear and process information over the phone which isn't always the case.

We learn early on in our medical school training that giving even a young person a bad diagnosis will essentially end the conversation. Their brain is instantly elsewhere. Further "communication" will have to be done at a later time.

Miss-Hearing

The purpose of making these observations is to simply point out that much of what we say and/or mean is not being heard or understood. There is a parlor game which most people have played that involves having a number of people sitting in a circle. Player one whispers something to player two. Player two whispers the "same thing" to player three and so forth. By the time the item gets to player ten, nothing is accurate.

Another major problem with communication has to do with definitions. Frequently, people will use words or phrases assuming that everyone agrees on the definitions or meanings. This may or may not be the case. This is the famous "apples" and "oranges" dilemma.

Is there anything that can be done about this? I will attempt to address this in the section titled "solutions."

Chapter 10

Family

Traditional

I GREW UP in a "traditional family." My parents met on a "blind date." My father's roommate introduced him to his girlfriend's sister. They dated for several years while my father was finishing his schooling. When my father got his first job and a steady income, they married.. My father was a professor at the University of Minnesota. My mother was a homemaker with a college degree in Home Economics. The families in the neighborhood were all very similar. The fathers went to work, the mothers stayed home. The mothers were usually home when the kids came home from school. No one was divorced or even seemed to be "having problems." We lived in a world of "nuclear families." Everyone seemed happy and content. The parents socialized and the kids played together. Many of the fathers were employed by the University of Minnesota.

Men's Work, Women's Work

My father was the "bread winner." He also took care of the car and the repairs around the house and did the "heavy things" that needed to be done. When my brother and I were old enough, we took care of the yard and garden with some help from both parents. We, also, were responsible for taking of the dishes after a meal.

My mother did the cooking, cleaning, shopping and bill paying along with all the other things that mothers do. She was always home when we came home from school and was the one who went to the PTA and other school activities.

My father rarely cooked except for his breakfast. That was at least partly because he got up early to go to work. He did do some barbecuing once in a while but the kitchen was basically my mother's domain. My brother and I would occasionally help her and would also cook once in a while but not often. When my mother was sick, however, my dad did take over the domestic responsibilities. I don't remember my father ever being sick, so I'm not sure how that would have worked. I'm sure my mother would have figured it out.

My point in mentioning these things is to indicate that from my standpoint, my parents had designated "tasks" which they performed. Both worked very hard at those things they did. There was parity as far as the work load was concerned.

The Modern Life

In today's world, things are very different. Frequently, both husbands and wives are working outside the home. This requires a different division of labor on the home front. Many wives feel that they have a bigger share of the work load than their husbands and this can understandably lead to conflict and frustration. Watching young couples in action, however, it looks to me as if most husbands do share in many of the tasks which used to be done only be women.

Being Number 1

In the summer, my brother and I had to work four hours each morning in the yard. The rest of the day was ours. Our allowance was 10 cents a week and 5 cents went to church. We earned our "spending" money by delivering newspapers and mowing and weeding lawns and yards for neighbors.

We were quite different personality wise and also enjoyed very different extracurricular activities but it seemed that we were both #1 in our parents' eyes.

It seems to me that everyone needs to feel as if they are the "most important" at some time in their lives. If they don't get this from their parents, they need to get it elsewhere. Maybe this is the reason for gangs and "groupies." Also, it may be the reason for marital problems. If a man or woman needs to be #1, that may work until kids come along. If the man needs to be #1, his wife could be so occupied with the child or children that he will seek "being #1" elsewhere. If it's the wife, she may be unable to provide the necessary emotional stability for the kids or she may even end up leaving the raising of the kids to someone else.

If husband or wife #1 doesn't provide the necessary attention, they may look for it outside the marriage or in husband or wife #2 or even #3.

My brother and I have discussed this, and neither one of us can remember ever wondering whether we were loved or not. We never even thought about it. We never felt unloved.

Homebodies

We both ended up living at home until our mid-twenties because we were both in school and single. It made perfect economic sense to stay at home because we lived a mile from the St. Paul campus. We also really enjoyed being with our parents and they, also, seemed to enjoy having us around. Our mother continued to wash our clothes and make meals when we were home. My brother and I both paid for our educations and all other "incidentals." We both had lived "independently" and could certainly take care of ourselves but it made more sense to stay "at home." We always assumed that what we did was perfectly "normal." In recent years, I've learned that it was actually strange that we wanted to, or were "allowed" to, stay at home all those years. Also, it appears that there is frequently conflict between parents and children and the "prevailing wisdom" is that such conflict is a necessary part of "growing up" and "breaking away." Not doing this can "create" many problems later in life. Maybe that explains a lot! I never had that. Neither did my brother.

Based on my "upbringing" and watching the issues which seem to be prevalent in disrupted families, including my own, I'm a strong believer in maintaining a nuclear family if at all possible. Divorces should not be "taken lightly" especially if there are children involved.

Issues and Bad Assumptions

What came to light later in my life was the fact that my mother didn't think my father loved her. She even said that if divorce had been accepted the way it is now, she would have divorced him! My father adored my mother. He would have been totally distressed if he had known that she thought he didn't. He was doing everything men do to show their love. He worked hard, he took care of the house, the car, the yard and made sure that we were physically and financially safe and secure.

He was, however, not very physically or emotionally demonstrative—most men weren't in those days. In light of this and what I now know, I can certainly see how she could have come to her conclusion.

I can't imagine what would have happened to my brother and me if our parents had divorced! If it had happened, it would have been because of a wrong assumption!

Some Aspects of One Divorce

I thought about committing suicide when I was going through my first divorce. From my standpoint, I was "losing" everything that really mattered to me. I was living in a grungy apartment and told when and where I could see my kids and was seemingly being "beaten up" by everyone. I still was expected to work hard and "provide" for my wife as well as the kids. My wife told me she never loved me and was "forced" to marry me. I felt betrayed and society didn't seem to care. Only my friends, family and work kept me going. Also, I realized that my kids would need me for all sorts of reasons, not only then, but in the future. So, I didn't take my life. But I certainly thought about it more than once.

In retrospect, my wife may actually have felt she was "forced" to marry me at the time of the marriage or maybe this was an "afterthought" if she felt unloved or unsafe during the marriage. Unloved and/or unsafe—just like many wives apparently feel. The sad thing, from my standpoint, was that I did love her. I still do. But, I was very busy professionally and I'm sure didn't show or express my feelings as much or as often as I should have. I, also, probably didn't listen very well to her issues and concerns. I was a typical man.

Chapter 11

Fathers & Daughters, Mothers & Sons

For Emphasis

THIS CHAPTER MAY be the most important and meaningful in this entire work. If for no other reason than to reveal that it's something I got totally wrong.

Fathers and Daughters–Part 1

Who is the most important person in a young girl's life? My assumption has always been that it was her mother. It turns out that this is quite often wrong. Frequently, if not always, it's her father. Most men I've talked with don't realize this. Our assumptions are again incorrect.

When my daughter was 13, she moved in with me. I assumed that this was because she liked Spokane better than California and had many friends here. It never dawned on me that she was here because of me.

She was having some of the typical teenage girl issues and I didn't understand her appearance and behavior in the least. Consequently, we had our "issues." Because of this, she didn't think I loved her. She could certainly give you examples of my comments and behavior to support her position. That position just happens to be wrong. Unbeknownst to me, she was so distressed that she even thought about committing suicide. She presumably felt this way at least partly because "even her father didn't love her." If your father doesn't love you, who will? Kids apparently have a hard time distinguishing between "like" and "love." My actions were interpreted to mean that I neither liked nor loved her. Bad result! This has been a very hard assumption to overcome. It's only been recently that she realizes that there is a clear difference and that she has always been loved.

Fathers and Daughters–Part 2

I've asked many women who the most important person was in their lives as they were growing up. They almost always say it was their father. If they say it was someone other than their father, I will ask them where their father fit into the picture. They will usually indicate that he was either absent or so busy that they rarely had much contact with him. Occasionally, women have indicated that they were frightened of their fathers for a variety of reasons. On further questioning, they almost always indicate that they adored their dads and that they always wanted to have that "special" relationship.

I've asked many men with daughters who the most important person in their daughter's life was as she was growing up. It's rare that the father will indicated that it was him. They almost always indicated that it was the mother.

The upshot of this is that men need to assume that they are the most important person in their daughter's lives and act accordingly. Daughters need to know that they are, and always will be, loved-even if we have trouble figuring out their behavior. One thing that all fathers do know is that their daughters have them wrapped around their little fingers! I suspect that daughters know this too. Feeling loved, however, is different than feeling in control.

Mothers and Sons–Part 1

It may actually be that the most important person in a young man's life is his mother. I'm less clear regarding this but considering the father—daughter issue, it certainly requires consideration. When I was growing up both parents were very important and both played out their roles very well. Both parents were "special" in their own ways and there was a special bond for both of them. I do know, however, that my mother was the one I really talked to about everything. I talked to my dad when I needed help or advice.

I, also, do know that there is a very special bond between my son and his mother and that this appears to be the case for most other sons and mothers as well.

I can see why many mothers may feel exploited and unappreciated. Kids can be worse than husbands at expressing love and appreciation. All my mother wanted was a hug. How often did I hug her unless she asked? Keep in mind that, from a woman's standpoint, if she has to ask it doesn't count! That even applies to mothers and sons.

Mothers and Sons–Part 2

How, then, do I know that men love and respect their mothers. I know because of Monday Night Football!

If you have ever watched Monday Night Football or any other football game on television, you have seen the running back, or the quarter back, or the end or the safety score a touchdown.

After scoring, they celebrate and then go over to the bench and sit down. The camera zooms in on them and they look up at the camera, wave, and they say…? It's virtually always the case. It never seems to fail. For those of you who don't watch football, what they say is: "Hi Mom!" It's rarely, if ever, is "Hi Dad!"

We just never, or rarely, say those things or do those things that mean so much to our mothers when we should. And, it's so simple!

Some Action Items

Is there a solution? I would argue that there is. We just need to be reminded. At least boys do. What if school teachers reminded the kids as they left their last class to give their moms a big hug and a kiss when they got home? What if the school bus drivers said the same thing when the kids got off the bus? What about Sunday school teachers? What about the newspaper?

So what? Presumably kids are committing suicide or thinking about committing suicide because they feel things are just as hopeless as I did and my daughter did. Perhaps they also feel unloved or unsafe. That would make sense to me. So, maybe it will make a difference if we go out of our way to make sure that the kids know they are loved and safe even if their behavior, at the time, may be less then we, as parents, would like to see. I know that my parents didn't always approve of the things I did. But, I never felt "unloved" or "unsafe."

Chapter 12

Why Don't Our Relationships Work?

Relationships Are Many and Often Challenging

A LL "RELATIONSHIPS" CAN be challenging. We are never without relationships. In addition to family, they involve friends, employment, neighbors, countries, religious organizations, classmates, etc. Since this work is focused on men/women relationships, the balance of this section will be devoted to that topic exclusively. But, the issue is everywhere.

Decreasing the Risk of Failure?

As has been indicated, marriage is considered by many to be the most important decision we make in our lives and this clearly involves a relationship. Yet, we are allowed to do it without training or testing. Anyone of age and with enough money to buy a marriage license can do it.

Why don't we let people do anything else they want with such a minimum requirement? Why do we require that virtually everyone demonstrate a certain level of proficiency before they are allowed to do things? What if someone wanted to be a school teacher or dentist or doctor or accountant or attorney or hair dresser or engineer and all they had to do was be over 18 and pay $20.00?

Some relationships are clearly at risk early on. Books have been written about "personalities to avoid" when involved in any relationship but certainly when anticipating marriage. Perhaps the MMPI or some other psychological test should be a required test before being able to get a marriage license so that these personality issues don't come into play. For now, I'll assume that's not going to be happening.

There is obviously something that brings people together in elective relationships like friendships and marriages. There has to be some type of "chemistry" and this type of chemistry is not just with everyone. When these relationships fail, something has to affect that chemistry.

A Relationship Ends – What Went Wrong?

When relationships end it's always for the same reason. It's the lack of the one thing all parents want for their kids. That one "thing" is happiness. People are unhappy for one reason. That reason is that their needs aren't being met. It's often said that it takes two people to cause the end of a marriage. I would argue that technically it only takes one. Only one person needs to file for a divorce. That person is the "unhappy" one which means that their needs aren't being met. This may come as a total surprise to the other person because their needs are quite possibly being met.

The main factor in a good relationship is trust. If something happens to trust, things deteriorate in a hurry and will never be quite the same. Consequently, to keep relationships healthy, everything possible must be done to maintain that trust. We tend to get lazy and assume that everything is fine

Focus on Communication

Typically, there is a breakdown in "communication."

My first wife clearly sensed this. At her insistence, we went to a weekend program called "Marriage Encounter." For those of you unfamiliar with this program, it involves a weekend away from home with other married couples and the exercise involves writing letters to your spouse. It is church sponsored and, therefore, has significant religious overtones.

I went but not willingly. I had "better" things to do. The experience wasn't really all that bad but the intent was to have the daily letter writing continue after the weekend. After a long, hard day at the office and hospitals, I was less than enthusiastic about writing letters. Consequently, things soon reverted to "normal." It seemed to me that things were OK and letter writing took a lot of extra time and work. Why not just talk?

The obvious problem with this is that it requires language and now we're back in that arena. Different languages!

Still, some people are much better at this than others. There are many clichés regarding the requirements to maintain a "happy" marriage. Among these are:

- It's not 50/50. It's 80/80!
- Never go to bed mad.
- It requires constant effort.
- It requires falling in love over and over. Always with the same person.

Chapter 13

Solutions

Where Do We Go From Here?–Part 1

Is there anything that can be done about all of this? The simple answer is "I don't know." When I reflect back on my own experiences, I would like to think that knowing "then" some of the things I know "now" couldn't have hurt. As is true for most people, I've grown to soon old and too late smart.

To start with, if it's accurate that marriage is the most important decision we make in our lives, there should at least be time and energy given to educating everyone starting at an early age about the fact that there are differences between men and women and how they think and communicate. It should, at least, be known that we speak different languages.

I would like to think that if there had been classes in school or Sunday school about these differences, I would have at least listened.

The whole issue of assumptions could certainly be addressed repeatedly in school as well as at home if only to demonstrate that everyone continually makes them but that they are frequently incorrect and should always be viewed with this in mind.

Where Do We Go From Here?–Part 2

I would suggest that all people are basically good and aren't trying to inflict pain in any way. Why would they? Why would they want to hurt someone they love? Why would they want to hurt anyone period? If you categorize divorced couples, it's rare that there is a "bad guy." Typically women will support the woman and men will support the man and families will "stick together" but if one is truly objective both people are basically okay.

Whether or not taking a strange test like the MMPI would have better helped me make permanent relationship choices is also intriguing. Would anyone marry, or not marry, someone if a skilled and experienced person suggested that you were not well suited based on a very strange test? Or even if the person you "loved" and wanted to marry had one of the "personalities to avoid"?

Perhaps getting a marriage license should require passing a "test" of some kind and possibly even require some professional counseling.

Some Useful Topics For Discussion

I don't claim that what's been discussed thus far is always correct but it seems to be at least part of the time and, if nothing else, offers some topics of conversation.

1) Communication is the main ingredient for maintaining relationships.

2) Men and women speak different languages.

3) Women often assume men marry for sex and to be "taken care of."

4)	Men actually usually marry for love. They don't need to be "taken care of" and "sex" is, and always has been, available outside of marriage.

5)	"Love," at least for men, involves some strange chemistry which often occurs "slam dunk." Once this happens the man is a "gone goose."

6)	"Love" for women may be different and seems to involve pragmatic considerations.

7)	"Love" is essential but not sufficient for a happy long lasting relationship. i.e. It doesn't always result in marriage or a happy marriage. More is required.

8)	Women may sense and experience "love" in ways different than men.

9)	Women need to be shown that they're loved in special but simple ways. Men don't know this.

10)	Men don't need to have love expressed the same way women do.

11)	Women need to be shown they're loved over and over again. Every day doesn't hurt.

12)	Men need to be reminded of point 11). Our brains don't work that way!

13)	Everybody needs to know that they are loved and cared for. Everybody!!

14)	Both men and women appear to have a biological need to love and care for someone or something.

15)	Kids have a hard time distinguishing between "like" and "love."

16)   People make "wrong assumptions" continuously based on "facts."

17)   These "wrong assumptions" are frequently very destructive in all sorts of ways.

18)   Men's and women's brains "think" in different ways. Neither way is "better."

19)   Everyone needs to feel safe.

20)   Men tease people they really like. Women don't and teasing can hurt.

21)   Women want men to look at them when their talking. Men can have a hard time doing this.

22)   Women don't want solutions when they complain. Men do.

23)   Women like to be held. Men like to hold the woman they love.

24)   Fathers may be the most important people in their daughters' lives.

25)   Mothers may be the most important people in their sons' lives.

26)   If a woman has to ask, it doesn't count.

27)   Men are "simple."

28)   Women are "complicated."

29)   "Making love" for men is a very special way of showing love. For women, being held may actually be more important than "making love."

Chapter 14

Summary Remarks

Caring Enough to Care

IF I REALLY want to "surprise" a patient, all I need to do is call them to see "how they're doing." They simply can't believe a doctor would do such a thing. I'm constantly thinking about and "fussing" about my patients. Especially, the ones I'm puzzled by or who are having tough times with their health issues. If I had the time, I would be calling many of them regularly. Obviously, I can't. That doesn't mean I don't care. In many ways, they are my responsibility. The same applies to my family and friends. People need to know that they are cared about. It's not that hard. We just need to "know the rules."

The "Rules"

The "rules" are few and simple:

> Wives need to realize their husbands love them. That's why they married them! They didn't marry them for "sex" or to be "taken care of."

Husbands need to show their wives they love them *every day*. They need to *remind themselves* that this is needed. It's simple!

Kids need to know that their parents love them and always will. That just won't change! They also need to understand that their behavior can affect how well their parents "like" them. But that is very different than "love" and it's "love" that really counts because it lasts forever. "Like" can change in an instant.

Nearly Closing Comments

We're all in this "mess" together. If we don't take care of each other who will? Obviously, this applies first and foremost to our families and then to our friends. But, it really applies to everyone. "It takes a village to raise a child." It takes a community to keep the community intact.

If all these "solutions" are ineffective and all else fails and divorce appears to be the only option left and children are involved, I would only hope that ultimately attorneys will be taken out of play. They only make a horrible situation worse.

Chapter 15

Closing Observations

The Condensed Contents–1

A S WAS INDICATED in the introduction, the intent of this work was to attempt to determine if there was some way to have an impact on the number of failed relationships/marriages with all the attending consequences. The main premise is that we are all alike and based on that certain behavioral consistencies will be present.

There is clearly a "hard-wired need" for men and women to be together with the obvious desire to procreate. Society has determined, at least traditionally, that this should involve marriage. Who we marry is arguably the most important decision we make during our lifetime and yet we make this decision with very little if any preparation or education. We come together and are expected to know what to do. When needs are not met, people become disillusioned, hurt and angry which leads to disruption of the marriage either with or without divorce. Since children are frequently involved, the disruption becomes much more complicated and painful.

The Condensed Contents–2

When I went through my first divorce, there were many "experts" who indicated that "kids are tough" and that it is better to have a divorce than it is to have a persistent unhappy marriage. I'm never quite sure where "experts" get their "facts," but I can tell you that I learned early on during the divorce proceedings that my kids weren't "tough." Everyone was struggling but the kids' safety and security was totally disrupted and trying to explain to them what was happening was impossible. It's said that in these situations, the kids blame themselves and I think that there was certainly an element of this. Once the attorneys were involved it was "war" which is probably always the case. An "amicable divorce" appears to me to be the ultimate oxymoron.

Was there anything that could have been done to prevent all of this? Was the selection process totally flawed? Were "personalities to avoid" in play? Once the relationship was at risk, was there anything that could or should have been done?

The Condensed Contents–3

The suggestions that I have made involve having some type of required education and possibly counseling before anyone is allowed to get a marriage license. Possibly, even offering psychological testing to see if people are "well matched." Possibly, even requiring a probation period from the purchase date of the license until one can actually "tie the knot." This is actually in place in the State of Washington but it's almost "after the fact." People have to wait three months after a divorce is final before they can re-marry.

It's not that people don't go through divorces and survive. They do and quite often they are ultimately very happy and content. Some people may even suggest that they are much better people for the experience. Life is too short to be unhappy.

I don't want anyone who's read this work to think that I'm miserable and unhappy. I'm actually very happy and content, but I think life would have been easier and more secure for my kids if this wasn't part of their "curriculum vitae." What all parents want for their kids is happiness and divorces can make that harder to acquire.

The Bottom Line

If the content of this work saves even one marriage, I will be very satisfied.

www.ingramcontent.com/pod-product-compliance
Lightning Source LLC
Chambersburg PA
CBHW060203290526

45789CB00003B/1140